DISCUSSION GUIDE

RESPECTABLE
SINS

This discussion guide is designed to accompany the book *Respectable Sins: Confronting the Sins We Tolerate* by Jerry Bridges. For best participation and life application, it is strongly recommended that every group participant have his or her own copy of both the book and discussion guide. Additional copies are available at your Christian bookseller or from NavPress (1-800-366-7788 or www.navpress.com).

DISCUSSION GUIDE

RESPECTABLE SINS

CONFRONTING THE SINS WE TOLERATE

JERRY BRIDGES

Discussion Guide by Stephen Sorenson

NAVPRESS

Discipleship Inside Out™

Discipleship Inside Out™

NavPress is the publishing ministry of The Navigators, an international Christian organization and leader in personal spiritual development. NavPress is committed to helping people grow spiritually and enjoy lives of meaning and hope through personal and group resources that are biblically rooted, culturally relevant, and highly practical.

For a free catalog go to www.NavPress.com
or call 1.800.366.7788 in the United States or 1.800.839.4769 in Canada.

ISBN-13: 978-1-60006-207-0

Cover design by www.studiogearbox.com
Cover image by Jupiter Images
Creative Team: Don Simpson, Darla Hightower, Arvid Wallen, Pat Reinheimer

Some of the anecdotal illustrations in this book are true to life and are included with the permission of the persons involved. All other illustrations are composites of real situations, and any resemblance to people living or dead is coincidental.

Unless otherwise identified, all Scripture quotations in this publication are taken from the *English Standard Version* (ESV), copyright © 2001 by Crossway Bibles, a division of Good News Publishers. Used by permission. All rights reserved. Other versions used include: the *HOLY BIBLE: NEW INTERNATIONAL VERSION*® (NIV®), Copyright © 1973, 1978, 1984 by International Bible Society, used by permission of Zondervan Publishing House, all rights reserved; and *THE MESSAGE* (MSG). Copyright © 1993, 1994, 1995, 1996, 2000, 2001, 2002, 2005. Used by permission of NavPress Publishing Group.

Printed in the United States of America

10 11 12 / 14

To fellow travelers everywhere — May we discover together the encouragement and hope that is ours in Jesus Christ and bring honor to His name as we face up to the "respectable" sins.

Contents

Confronting the Sins
We Tolerate

S ome years ago a book was published with the title *I'm OK, You're OK*. In contrast to that book title, the attitude of many Christians seems to be "I'm OK and You're Not." That is, we seem to be good at seeing other people's sins but not our own. We see and bemoan the flagrant sins of our culture, and we're even quick to point out the sins of our brothers and sisters in Christ, but we are often blind to the more subtle sins that we tolerate in our own lives — those I call "respectable" sins.

You and I may actually be doing quite well when it comes to avoiding the more overt sins. But what about the more subtle ones — the "respectable" sins that can still hinder our walks with God and harm our relationships with others? God has made clear in His Word that He is as dishonored and displeased by our anxiety, unthankfulness, frustration, selfishness, impatience, and discontentment as He is by the overt sins we're so proud to avoid.

In an effort to help us face and deal with these "subtle" sins, I have written *Respectable Sins: Confronting the Sins We Tolerate*. This discussion guide is a companion to that book. I commend it to you as invaluable not only for small-group interaction but also for your own personal study and growth in Christ.

Through experience I have found that we often need more than to merely have our own sins — even the "respectable" ones that we tend to minimize — pointed out to us. We need encouragement and hope, and these come only through the gospel. The good news of Jesus Christ *encourages* us in our personal struggles with sin because it assures us that in our standing with God, He has already forgiven our sins through the death of His Son on the cross. The gospel gives us *hope* because it also promises to us the power of the Holy Spirit to enable us to deal with our sins. We need both assurances. We cannot effectively deal with the expressions of our subtle sins until we know they are forgiven. And we cannot effectively deal with our sins apart from the help of the Holy Spirit.

As you use this guide, you will find that I emphasize both of these gospel truths. So do not approach this study with the fear that it will only reveal sin and leave you to wallow in it. Rather, you will find both hope in the gospel and practical suggestions for dealing with your sins. And lest you think that I have written from the perspective of "I'm OK and You're Not," let me assure you that I must deal with many of these sins myself. So together let's confront the subtle sins we tolerate in our lives and implement God's wonderful plan for redemption and victory.

Jerry Bridges

Tips for Personal and Group Study

This guide has been thoughtfully prepared to enrich your reading, discussion, and personal application of *Respectable Sins* by best-selling author Jerry Bridges. We call it a "discussion guide" because it stimulates meaningful interaction in small groups, Bible studies, and Christian growth classes, but it also encourages each participant's individual understanding and application of the life-changing principles found in *Respectable Sins*. So the guide you hold in your hands serves three important purposes: (1) it's a road map to enable the group facilitator; (2) it's a reading and application guide for the group member; and (3) it's a discussion guide to enhance the group-interaction experience.

IF YOU'RE A GROUP MEMBER

If you're a participant, you'll need your own copy of both the book and this guide. You'll be prompted to read specific chapters of the book before each group session and respond to the "Think It Through" personal-study questions for that session. The quality of your personal reading and preparation will help to ensure quality interaction when you get together to discuss what you have read.

As you read *Respectable Sins*, keep pen in hand and feel free to underline passages or put stars or question marks in the margins, noting any principles or insights that stand out to you. We know you're going to enjoy the book and grow in your faith as you sit at the feet of one of the world's most beloved authors and Bible teachers.

After you've read the assigned chapters of *Respectable Sins*, you'll go to the second page of each session in this guide and respond to the "Think It Through" questions. These will help you process some of the key points you've just read. Some questions ask you to look up and respond to selected Bible passages. We strongly encourage you to engage fully with these personal-study opportunities, but if your time is limited and you're able to read only the book chapters before group time, you can come back to the "Think It Through" section later.

At the end of each session you'll find a page titled "Take It to Heart." This page is for you to journal your personal reflections, action points, and prayers in response to the week's reading and discussion. Following the group discussion, find a place of solitude, quiet your heart before God, and then write your responses to the guided Personal Reflection, Personal Action Points, and Personal Prayer prompts we've provided for you. You may find that these journaling exercises are the most meaningful to you of the entire study-and-discussion experience.

IF YOU'RE THE GROUP FACILITATOR

If you have the honor of facilitating this group-study experience, the rest of this section will help you guide your group through an enriching time of discovery.

First things first, you'll want to be sure each participant has his or her own copy of both the book and the discussion guide. In many small groups, participants are willing to pitch in for the purchase price, and the facilitator makes the actual purchase. A married couple may be okay with sharing a single copy of *Respectable Sins* between them, but as you'll soon see, the discussion guides are personal. Participants will be writing their own responses not only to study questions but also to personal-reflection questions. Be sure you've done an accurate head count, then visit your Christian bookseller (or contact NavPress at 1-800-366-7788 or www .navpress.com) for the necessary quantity of books and discussion guides.

Now for your road map to help facilitate each group session.

1. It goes without saying, but we'll say it anyway, that you should be thoroughly familiar with the material before each group session. This means you're committed to reading the assigned book chapters ahead of time, working through the "Think It Through" personal-study questions, and reviewing the "Talk It Over" discussion questions.

2. Bathe your personal preparation, and each upcoming group session, in prayer. Pray for God's wisdom, guidance, and sensitivity as you prepare and facilitate. Pray for His profound work in the heart and life of each participant.

3. Each session specifies the chapters in *Respectable Sins* to be read "Before Gathering." You'll want to call attention to the next session's assigned readings at the close of each meeting. Participants are also encouraged to work through the corresponding "Think It Through" personal-study questions in their discussion guides prior to each group session.

4. On the left page preceding each session of the guide you'll find a "Progress Report" box — a quick personal-application review of some of the key principles of the previous session. Start each group experience by posing these questions and encouraging participants to share their personal discoveries and/or spiritual progress. You'll all be encouraged as you hear what your friends are learning!

5. After the progress report, have everyone follow along as one group member reads aloud the "Get Focused" section. This underscores the importance of the chapters they've read during the week and sets the tone for the coming discussion.

6. Take a few minutes to ask for questions or insights participants may have gained in their study of the "Think It Through" section during the week. (Tip: Preselect a couple of the questions and insights to highlight in case people did not complete this section.)

7. Devote the bulk of the discussion time to the "Talk It Over"

questions designed for group discussion. Vary your approach: For some questions you might pose the issue to no one in particular and wait for responses. For others, you might direct the question to a specific individual, let him or her respond, and then encourage others to respond as well. As much as time permits, encourage unrushed, multiple responses. Sometimes you'll discover deeper levels of insight as one participant builds upon the thoughts of another.

8. Encourage participants to take the time to enjoy the personal journaling experience provided at the end of each session. Responding to the guided prompts in these "Take It to Heart" segments will enhance their personal understanding and life application of the principles you've discussed.

9. Take a moment to point out the "For Next Time" assignments for the next session. For the best learning experience, we encourage participants to make quality time to read the assigned chapters and respond to the corresponding "Think It Through" personal-study questions. However, you may want to assure them that if they can read only the assigned book chapters, that's fine — they can dig in to the "Think It Through" section some other time.

10. Conclude by praying together. We've provided suggested topics under "Group Prayer" to get prayer time started. You can have one person pray or open it up for brief conversational prayers from anyone who wishes to pray aloud. (Tip: No one should ever feel pressured or obligated to pray aloud. It can help relax everyone if you assure them of this rule ahead of time.)

Oh, and one more thing. *Have fun!* Sure, it's a serious topic. And yes, you have a serious responsibility. But inhale, exhale, relax, and enjoy the experience. Approach your preparation as well as each group session with a positive, expectant spirit. Do your very best and leave the results to God. (Tip: *That's* when the fun really starts!)

May God richly bless you, and your group, as you read and discover His blessings together.

The Editors

Before the First Session

Prior to session 1, make sure each participant has his or her own copies of *Respectable Sins* and the *Respectable Sins Discussion Guide*. Encourage everyone to read chapters 1, 2, and 3 of the book and then respond to the "Think It Through" personal-study questions on the second page of session 1 in this guide.

If you are distributing the books and discussion guides at your initial group meeting, have someone read chapter 1 aloud as the group follows along. Encourage participants to point out insights or discoveries that stood out to them. Talk together about why it's important to face up to the truth when it comes to the "respectable" sins in our lives. Pray together for open hearts and minds, and for a spirit of mutual encouragement, as you study and discuss the book during the coming weeks. Then assign the "Prior to Session 1" preparation (above) for your next meeting — the real "session 1" of this study.

Facing Up to the Truth

(Chapters 1, 2, and 3)

BEFORE GATHERING: Read *Respectable Sins* chapters 1, 2, and 3, then respond to the "Think It Through" questions that begin on the next page of this guide.

KEY VERSE: "Sin is lawlessness." (1 John 3:4)

GET FOCUSED

Some forms of cancer grow undetected until they reach a terminal stage. Likewise, sin — especially the so-called "acceptable" or "subtle" sins — can exist in our lives, virtually undetected and dangerous. We can be deceived into believing that such sin is not all that bad, into denying that sin is really sin, and into not thinking about sin. In fact, the word *sin* has virtually disappeared from our culture — and is even avoided in some churches. Well-intentioned believers find it all too easy to focus on the blatant sins of our "evil" culture while ignoring their own, more-subtle sins — "respectable" sins.

In contrast to the feel-good-about-ourselves philosophy of our day, Puritan believers in the seventeenth century had a different view of themselves and sin. They feared the reality of sin; they saw all sin as a diabolical force living within themselves. They recognized, like the biblical writers, that *any* sin breaks God's law.

During this session we will explore the impact of sins that Christians tend to downplay in their own lives—sins such as impatience, gossip, pride, resentment, and anger. These often become larger malignancies, cascading us into deeper sinfulness.

Yes, God sent Jesus to earth to take humankind's sins on Himself. But as long as we believers recognize our call to glorify God and become like Jesus, we will battle sin. To live as God's people includes facing sin—especially sin we don't recognize or we rationalize away. That's what this first session is all about.

THINK IT THROUGH

For Personal Study

I. WHAT IS SIN?

1. Why do you think it's important for us to understand what sin is and its impact on our lives and relationships?

2. What do James 1:14-15 and 2:10-11 reveal about the root of our sinful actions? About God's law and the consequences of breaking it?

3. In Matthew 5:22,27-28, what did Jesus emphasize concerning the seriousness of sin—of breaking God's law?

II. What Happened to the Word *Sin*?

1. What evidence do you see that the word *sin* has virtually disappeared from our culture? That awareness of personal sin has effectively disappeared from many believers' consciences? Explain your answer.

2. What impact do you think the "softening" of language regarding sin is having on our lives? On our churches?

What's Become of Sin?

The very word, *sin*, which seems to have disappeared, was once a proud word. It was once a strong word, an ominous and serious word. . . . But the word went away. It has almost disappeared—the word, along with the notion. Why? Doesn't anyone sin anymore? Doesn't anyone believe in sin?

Karl Menninger
Whatever Became of Sin?*

3. Why is it often easier for believers to focus on the sins of unbelievers rather than on their own personal sins?

---

* Karl Menninger, MD, *Whatever Became of Sin?* (New York: Hawthorne Books, 1973), 14–15.

III. "RESPECTABLE" SINS

1. List some common "respectable" sins. Why do you think we are more inclined to tolerate them?

2. In Galatians 3:10, what did the apostle Paul quote to emphasize the importance of obeying God's law? What might this reveal about the consequences of tolerating "seemingly minor sins"?

3. Even though God always makes a decisive change in every believer's heart, what does every believer face when he or she seeks to live in obedience to God? (See Galatians 5:17; James 1:14.)

4. Describe the choices Peter and Paul urge every true believer to make. (See Galatians 5:16; Ephesians 4:29; 1 Peter 2:11.)

IV. HOW OUR SIN AFFECTS GOD

1. Jerry writes: "When we sin we violate the law of God in any way, . . . we rebel against the sovereign authority and transcendent majesty of God. We commit 'cosmic treason.'" It is indeed cosmic treason." Do you agree or disagree with the concept of "cosmic treason"? Explain.

State of Denial?

Even though our [believers'] hearts have been renewed, even though we have been freed from the absolute dominion of sin, even though God's Holy Spirit dwells within our bodies, . . . sin still lurks within us and wages war against our souls. It is the failure to recognize the awful reality of this truth that provides the fertile soil in which our "respectable" or "acceptable" sins grow and flourish.

Chapter 3, *Respectable Sins*

2. How much do you think God knows about our sin? (See Psalm 139:1-4; 1 Corinthians 4:5.)

3. Read 2 Samuel 12:1-10, where Nathan the prophet spoke God's words to David, who had committed adultery with Bathsheba, murdered her husband, and lived in denial of his sin. What do we learn about denial? About sin in relation to God and His law?

4. What effect does sin have on the Holy Spirit — that is, God — who lives inside each believer? (See Ephesians 4:30.)

TALK IT OVER

For Group Discussion

1. Why should we take our "respectable" sins seriously?

2. How might we begin to see our own sins more clearly instead of focusing so much on other people's sins?

3. What impact do you think the "softening" of language regarding sin is having on our lives? On our churches?

4. As we realize that our sin is not only rebellion against God's sovereign authority but a despising of both His law and His person, how might we view sin differently?

5. How might what we learned today influence what we say, do, and/or think?

GROUP PRAYER

As a group, thank God for the opportunity to gather and explore this important topic. Ask Him to help you recognize "respectable" sins and to take them seriously.

❧ ❧

FOR NEXT TIME: Read *Respectable Sins*, chapters 4, 5, and 6, then respond to the "Think It Through" personal-study questions for session 2.

↑↑↑↑↑↑↑↑↑↑↑↑↑↑

Take It to Heart
A Personal-Growth Journal

Personal Reflection

During this session, what discoveries, quotations, or verses especially connected with you? Why?

What "respectable" sins might you be tolerating in your life?

In what ways might these sins be affecting your life, your relationships, and your relationship with God?

What do you think God wants you to learn from that situation?

Personal Action Point

What one insight regarding "respectable" sins would you like to begin applying to your spiritual journey this week? Write it down and commit it to the Lord.

Personal Prayer

Write a brief prayer to God about sin's lure and impact in your life — and your desire for Him to help you stand strong in the face of temptation.

↑↑↑↑↑↑↑↑↑↑↑↑↑↑

What have you discovered this week about "respectable" sins?

As you have begun to apply what you learned from session 1, what new choices have you made? What challenges have you faced?

In what ways has knowing God's view of all sin — including the more "acceptable" ones — influenced you this week?

The Remedy for Sin

(Chapters 4, 5, and 6)

BEFORE GATHERING: Read *Respectable Sins* chapters 4, 5, and 6, and then respond to the "Think It Through" personal-study questions that begin on the next page of this guide.

KEY VERSES: "Blessed are those whose lawless deeds are forgiven, and whose sins are covered; blessed is the man against whom the Lord will not count his sin." (Romans 4:7-8)

GET FOCUSED

The apostle Paul and John Newton (writer of the hymn "Amazing Grace") viewed themselves as great sinners who had a great Savior — Jesus Christ.

Before meeting Jesus, Saul (renamed Paul) persecuted believers (See Acts 7:54–8:3). Toward the end of his life, Paul described himself as "the very least of all the saints" (Ephesians 3:8) and a "blasphemer, persecutor, and insolent opponent [of Christ]" (1 Timothy 1:13). He also wrote, "Christ Jesus came into the world to save sinners, of whom I am the foremost" (1 Timothy 1:15).

John, a former slave trader and slave-ship captain, never forgot his slave-related sin but focused on Jesus. "My memory is nearly gone," John said at the end of his life, "but I remember . . . that I am a great

The Basis for Forgiveness

The only sin that can be successfully fought against is forgiven sin. We cannot begin to deal with the *activity* of sin in our lives until we have first dealt with its guilt. . . . God through Christ has dealt with our guilt. The *only* basis for God's forgiveness is the blood of Christ shed on the cross for us.

Chapter 4, *Respectable Sins*

sinner, and that Christ is a great Savior."*

As Paul and John grew Christlike, they became increasingly aware of, and sensitive to, their sin. They described themselves as sinners in the present tense — "I *am*," not "I *was*." "And," Jerry Bridges writes, "if you and I are to make any progress in dealing with the acceptable sins of our lives, we must say the same."

Perhaps you find it difficult to identify with the grievous sins Saul and John committed. But have you gossiped, harbored resentment, acted selfishly, or distrusted God? Sin is sin.

The only remedy for our sin lies in the forgiveness of sin Jesus can provide. "The good news that God no longer counts my sin against me," writes the author, ". . . seems too good to be true." But it's not! And the Holy Spirit helps us deal with our sin, directing our spiritual transformation.

THINK IT THROUGH

For Personal Study

I. AS FOLLOWERS OF CHRIST, WE'RE DELIVERED FROM SIN'S POWER

1. The moment we receive salvation through Christ, what does God do for us regarding the guilt and reigning power of sin? (See Romans 6:1-2; Colossians 1:13-14.)

---

* Brian H. Edwards, *Through Many Dangers: The Story of John Newton* (Welwyn, England: Eurobooks, 1980), 191.

2. What does God use to convict us of our sins — including our selfishness and judgmental attitudes? (See 2 Timothy 3:16.)

He Won't Let Us Down

If we claim that we're free of sin, we're only fooling ourselves. . . . On the other hand, if we admit our sins — make a clean breast of them — he [God] won't let us down; he'll be true to himself. He'll forgive our sins and purge us of all wrongdoing.

1 John 1:8-9, MSG

3. What assurance do we have that, when we acknowledge our sinfulness and ask for God's forgiveness, He will forgive us and no longer hold our sin against us? (See Romans 4:7-8; Ephesians 1:7; 1 John 1:9.)

4. In Matthew 5:6, what did Jesus promise all who pursue righteousness, who earnestly desire to see their sin put to death and be replaced with the fruit of the Spirit? (See Matthew 5:4,6; Galatians 5:22-23.)

II. GOD HELPS EVERY BELIEVER DEAL WITH SIN

1. Read Galatians 5:16. What hope is promised as we seek to "put to death" sins that keep coming back? What does it mean to "walk by the Spirit"?

2. As we ask God to enable us to deal with our sin, what must we "store up" in our hearts? (See Psalm 119:11.)

3. How can we be sure that God the Father and the Son, working through the Holy Spirit who lives within every believer (see 1 Corinthians 6:19), will help us deal with sin and direct our spiritual transformation? (See Romans 8:31; Philippians 1:6; 2:12-13.)

4. What is the Holy Spirit doing within each believer? (See 2 Corinthians 3:18.)

TALK IT OVER

For Group Discussion

1. How does the truth that God has forgiven our sin free us to honestly and humbly face our sin?

2. What hinders us from recognizing our sin? Why do we allow sin to "reign" in our lives? (See Romans 6:12.)

3. How might our lives change if we consistently pray about subtle sins and ask for the Holy Spirit's help each time we encounter situations that might trigger these sins?

4. Why do we, in the author's words, "need to preach the gospel to ourselves," to read biblical assurances of God's forgiveness?

5. How should Jesus' work — the forgiveness that His death and resurrection accomplished — motivate us to deal with our sin?

The Holy Spirit's Role

Conviction of sin must be one of His [Holy Spirit's] vital works because we cannot begin to deal with a sin, especially one that is common and acceptable in our Christian culture, until we have first realized that the particular pattern of thought, word, or deed is indeed sin.

Chapter 5, *Respectable Sins*

GROUP PRAYER

Together, invite God to give each of you a heart that longs to be in intimate relationship with Him — and to promptly confess your sins as His Spirit makes you aware of them.

❧ ❧

FOR NEXT TIME: Read *Respectable Sins*, chapters 7 and 10, and then respond to the "Think It Through" questions for session 3.

****

TAKE IT TO HEART

A PERSONAL-GROWTH JOURNAL

PERSONAL REFLECTION

During this session, which insight(s) did you particularly appreciate and why?

If you trust Jesus Christ as your Savior and Lord, do you find it easy or difficult to comprehend God's forgiveness and infinite love for you? Why?

If you're a follower of Christ, God has completely forgiven your sin and will work with you to put to death expressions of sin in your life—including "respectable" ones. What does this mean to you personally?

PERSONAL ACTION POINT

In this space, write out 1 John 1:9 from your favorite translation of the Bible. Between now and the next session, memorize and reflect on this verse's personal promise.

PERSONAL PRAYER

Write out a brief prayer thanking God for the promise of 1 John 1:9 and what it means to you personally.

****

Share a few ways in which you are becoming more aware of "respect-able" sins and how to face them.

Have you tried asking for the Holy Spirit's help when you encoun-ter a situation that might trigger these sins? If so, what happened? If not, why not?

How would you describe the assurance you have that when you contritely confess your sin, God forgives you — no matter what sin you have committed? How is this assurance freeing you to honestly (and often) face up to your sin?

Ungodliness and Unthankfulness

(Chapters 7 and 10)

BEFORE GATHERING: Read *Respectable Sins* chapters 7 and 10, and then answer the "Think It Through" questions that begin on the next page of this guide.

KEY VERSES: "The grace of God has appeared, bringing salvation for all people, training us to renounce ungodliness. . . . Be filled with the Spirit, . . . giving thanks always and for everything to God the Father in the name of our Lord Jesus Christ." (Titus 2:11-12; Ephesians 5:18,20)

GET FOCUSED

Ungodliness is at the root of other "respectable" sins. All of us, to some degree, are ungodly. We live, at least occasionally, with little or no conscious thought of God — of God's will, God's glory, our dependence on God, or our responsibility to God. We forget that we live in the presence of the all-seeing, all-hearing God, who longs to be in intimate relationship with us.

Fortunately, God shows us how to deal with ungodliness. He wants us to glorify Him, to live lives worthy of Him and pleasing to Him — to let our light shine before others so they, too, may give glory to Him (see Matthew 5:16). He wants us to prayerfully desire an intimate relationship with Him that will permeate everything we think, say, and do. In this session, you'll learn about living in the awareness that all you are, have, and accomplish is by God's grace.

The other sin we'll examine today is *unthankfulness* toward God — not thanking Him for the many blessings He bestows on us, such as salvation, deliverance from spiritual darkness, and the gift of life. Everything we are and have is a gift from Him.

Even the ancient Israelites forgot to thank God for His spiritual and provisional blessings . . . with dire results. No wonder the apostle Paul wrote that we are to "[give] thanks always and for everything to God the Father in the name of our Lord Jesus Christ" (Ephesians 5:20). A spirit of thankfulness can transform your life!

THINK IT THROUGH

For Personal Study

I. DEALING WITH THE SIN OF UNGODLINESS

1. How is the definition of *ungodliness* in the quotation on page 35 different from what you thought *ungodliness* meant? What does Romans 1:18 reveal about this sin?

2. Do you agree or disagree that ungodliness is "apt to be the root cause of our other sins" and that each of us is guilty of this sin? Explain your answer.

3. Read James 4:13-15. For what expression of ungodliness did James, through the Holy Spirit, condemn those people?

4. What does Paul's summary prayer (Colossians 1:9-10) reveal about our responsibility to God? About our "typical," human-centered prayers for ourselves, friends, and family members?

What Is Ungodliness?

Ungodliness and wickedness are not the same. A person may be a nice, respectable citizen and still be an ungodly person. . . . Ungodliness describes an attitude toward God. Ungodliness may be defined as living one's everyday life with little or no thought of God, or of God's will, or of God's glory, or of one's dependence on God.

Chapter 7, *Respectable Sins*

II. DEALING WITH THE SIN OF UNTHANKFULNESS

1. During biblical times, leprosy devastated many lives. The Mosaic Law required that a leper continually cry out, "unclean, unclean" while walking along the road (Leviticus 13:45). In light of this, what is poignant about Jesus' experience between Samaria and Galilee? (See Luke 17:11-19.)

2. Read Romans 6:6,17 and Ephesians 2:1-5.

a. What is a person's spiritual condition without God?

b. What has God done for every believer?

3. According to Acts 17:24-25, why should we express heartfelt gratitude to God?

4. According to the promises of Romans 8:28-29,38-39, why should we give thanks by faith even when a situation is disappointing or difficult?

TALK IT OVER

For Group Discussion

1. Why do you think it's so easy for good people to be ungodly — to live most of the week as if God doesn't exist, as if they are not responsible to Him and dependent on Him?

2. If you feel comfortable doing so, share a time when you went through daily activities without even thinking of God. What impact did it have on your life or on those around you?

3. What practical things can we do each day to "train" ourselves "for godliness" (I Timothy 4:7) so we please and glorify God during even ordinary activities?

4. What are some blessings God has given you? Why is it important for us to thank Him for these blessings and make such thankfulness a natural part of our lives?

5. Review Romans 1:18-32, in which Paul vividly describes the downward moral spiral of pagan humanity. In verse 21, what does he emphasize regarding thankfulness, and what conclusions might we draw from this regarding our lives? Our culture?

6. Where does the faith come from to believe and thank God even in the midst of difficult circumstances? Describe a challenging time when you were — or were not — able to give thanks. What did God teach you through that experience?

GROUP PRAYER

As a group, ask God to kindle within each of you an even stronger desire to live a lifestyle of godliness and thankfulness.

❦ ❦

FOR NEXT TIME: Read *Respectable Sins* chapters 8 and 9, and then answer the questions in the "Think It Through" personal-study section for session 4.

✝✝✝✝✝✝✝✝✝✝✝✝✝✝

Take It to Heart
A Personal-Growth Journal

PERSONAL REFLECTION

Reread 1 Corinthians 10:31 and Matthew 5:16. To what extent are you mindful of doing "all" to the glory of God? How has ungodliness crept (or marched) into your social relationships . . . ordinary activities . . . your prayers . . . daily planning?

Do your words and actions demonstrate that you consciously and prayerfully seek to glorify God — or tend to forget about Him? What are your attitudes and actions communicating?

How much has God done for you in Christ? In what ways can you be sure to take time each day to thank God for His temporal provisions and spiritual blessings?

PERSONAL ACTION POINT

If God stood in front of you right now and told you to do *everything* to His glory, what changes would you immediately make in order to make Him the center focal point of your life?

PERSONAL PRAYER

Write out a brief prayer of commitment to the personal action points you listed above.

✝✝✝✝✝✝✝✝✝✝✝✝✝✝

How well did you do at consciously thinking about God? What helped you be more mindful of Him — His blessings, His will, His glory, your dependence on Him?

To what extent were you thankful to God — for unpleasant as well as great circumstances?

What challenges did you face in cultivating an attitude of thankfulness?

Anxiety, Frustration, and Discontentment

(Chapters 8 and 9)

BEFORE GATHERING: Read *Respectable Sins* chapters 8 and 9, and then respond to the "Think It Through" questions that start on the next page of this guide.

KEY VERSES: "[Cast] all your anxieties on him [God], because he cares for you. . . . All the days ordained for me were written in your book before one of them came to be." (1 Peter 5:7; Psalm 139:16, NIV)

GET FOCUSED

Each of us experiences pain and difficulties. Cars break down. Accidents hurt us or those we love. Relationships sour. Certainly you could list many examples. During this session, we'll consider three common "respectable" sins that often surface during painful or difficult times — anxiety, frustration, discontentment — and their considerable impact.

Anxiety (sometimes translated *worry*) shows up frequently in the Bible. Jesus often spoke about anxiety — once using this word six times in ten verses (See Matthew 6:25-34). ("Sister" words also show up often: "fear" and "afraid.") Why is anxiety — a fearful uncertainty over the future — among the "respectable" sins we're examining? Because when

If, Then

If all things are in his [God's] hand, if the very hairs of our head are numbered; if every event, great and small, is under the direction of his providence and purpose; and if he has a wise, holy, and gracious end in view . . . then we have nothing to do but with patience and humility to follow as he leads, and cheerfully to expect a happy issue.

JOHN NEWTON,
Letters of Newton*

we are anxious, we distrust God *and* we don't accept His sovereign orchestration of circumstances and events. We chafe under His providential will for our lives when it is different from our agendas.

Frustration usually involves becoming upset or even angry at whatever or whoever blocks our plans or desires. We forget that God's invisible hand is behind whatever triggers our frustration. As we'll see, whenever we face frustration we can rely on key resources and probably need to learn to pay attention to certain things.

Discontentment, which often arises from ongoing and unchanging circumstances we can do nothing about, is sinful when it negatively affects our relationship with God. How do we respond to Him when a job or marriage doesn't work out, we remain childless, chronic pain continues, or we face burdensome administrative details?

With the Holy Spirit's help, not only can we deal effectively with these sins as they crop up, but we can also experience more of God — and learn to trust Him no matter what circumstances we face.

THINK IT THROUGH

For Personal Study

I. ANXIETY AND FRUSTRATION

1. What did Jesus teach, in Matthew 6:25-34, about how believers should respond to anxiety (worry)?

---

* John Newton, *Letters of John Newton* (Carlisle, PA: The Banner of Truth Trust, 1960), 137.

2. What do Matthew 26:39 and Philippians 4:6-7 reveal about our need to pray for relief and deliverance from whatever tempts us to be anxious?

God Does Not Care?

When I give way to anxiety, I am, in effect, believing that God does not care for me and that He will not take care of me in the particular circumstance that triggers my anxiety of the moment. . . . Anxiety is a sin also because it is a lack of acceptance of God's providence in our lives . . . [His] orchestrating all circumstances and events in His universe for His glory and the good of His people.

Chapter 8, *Respectable Sins*

3. When our faith falters and our situations loom larger in our minds than God's promises, how should we obey Jesus' command in Matthew 6:34 and find hope in Luke 12:6? What insight does Mark 9:23-24 offer?

4. Our frustration, which usually involves being upset at whatever or whoever blocks our plans or desires, has roots in ungodliness because we are living as if God is not involved in our circumstances. What comforting and encouraging insights can we gain from Psalm 139:16 (NIV): "All the days ordained for me were written in your [God's] book before one of them came to be"?

II. DISCONTENTMENT

1. What is discontentment? When does it spur us to positive action — and when is it sinful?

2. Jerry writes, "It is our response to our circumstances rather than the degree of difficulty [in them] that determines whether or not we are discontent." Do you agree or disagree? Why?

3. One of the key verses for this session is Psalm 139:16. How might this verse help us in dealing with circumstances that tempt us to be discontented?

4. Write out what this statement from the author means to you: "We must believe that the Bible's teaching about these attributes [God's sovereignty, wisdom, goodness] really is true and that God has brought or allowed these difficult circumstances in our lives for His glory and our ultimate good."

TALK IT OVER

For Group Discussion

1. Why is anxiety so common in our culture — in our daily activities, in advertising, in news reports? How does the Bible's teaching about anxiety contradict what modern culture teaches about it?

2. Which other sins often crop up if we tolerate anxiety, frustration, and/or discontentment in our lives?

3. Do you think God sometimes allows us to face difficult, unchanging circumstances for reasons we may never know? Feel free to share a situation in which you learned a key lesson because you accepted that situation as part of God's plan for your life.

4. Discuss this quote from the author: "Suppose someone you love were to say to you, 'I don't trust you. I don't believe you love me and will care for me.' What an affront that would be to you! Yet that is what we are saying to God by our anxiety."

5. Throughout *Respectable Sins*, Jerry encourages us to remember God's attributes. If we believe and remember that God is infinitely wise, loving, and knows what is best for us, then how will we respond to circumstances that tempt us to be anxious, frustrated, and discontented? On the other hand, if we think God is simply toying with us and wanting us to suffer, how will we respond to trials?

GROUP PRAYER

In group prayer, thank God for making each of you more aware of "respectable" sins and their impact on your lives and relationships. Ask God for faith to believe that His providential will for you in all circumstances comes from His infinite wisdom and goodness — and is ultimately intended for your good.

❧ ❧

FOR NEXT TIME: Read *Respectable Sins* chapters 11 and 12, and then respond to the questions in the "Think It Through" personal-study section for session 5.

✦✦✦✦✦✦✦✦✦✦✦✦✦✦

Take It to Heart
A Personal-Growth Journal

Personal Reflection

What types of circumstances tempt you to become anxious, frustrated, and/or discontented?

When has God used your anxiety, frustration, and/or discontentment to teach you something, help you grow in a particular area, or get your attention and make you more attentive?

Which particular insights, quotations, or verses in session 4 especially connected with you? Why?

Personal Action Point

This next week, carefully note which circumstances tempt you to be anxious, frustrated, or discontented, and when temptation occurs, immediately ask God to help you trust and obey Him.

Personal Prayer

Write a prayer thanking God for being in control of your circumstances (even when you don't *feel* that certainty). Invite Him to help you respond in ways that serve and glorify Him.

✦✦✦✦✦✦✦✦✦✦✦✦✦✦

Since the last session, how did you do at trusting God with your anxieties and accepting His sovereign will?

If you became frustrated or discontented, what steps did you take? Or, what steps *should* you have taken?

In which specific area(s) have you noted progress?

Pride and Selfishness

(Chapters 11 and 12)

BEFORE GATHERING: Read *Respectable Sins* chapters 11 and 12, and then respond to the questions in the "Think It Through" personal-study section that starts on the next page of this guide.

KEY VERSES: "Love is patient and kind; love does not envy or boast; it is not arrogant or rude. It does not insist on its own way." (1 Corinthians 13:4-5)

GET FOCUSED

When we think of godly prayers, we certainly don't think of the self-righteous Pharisee's prayer in Luke 18:11: "God, I thank you that I am not like other men . . . or even like this tax collector." After all, the Bible emphasizes that God hates *sinful pride* and opposes proud people.

Ironically, each of us can develop a similar self-righteous attitude. It is often easy to see sinful pride in others but be blind to our own pride. That's why, in this session, we'll look at four expressions of pride that especially tempt believers: pride of moral self-righteousness, pride of correct doctrine, pride of achievement, and pride of an independent spirit.

Selfishness, the other "respectable" sin we'll explore, is also insidious and hard for us to recognize in ourselves. It crops up everywhere — even in the lives of theological heroes. We all have blind spots toward our selfishness. We are born with a sinful nature and are easily tempted to care more about our interests than those of other people. Though our selfishness may be crass and obvious, usually it is more delicate and refined because we care about what other people think. That's one reason we'll address not only selfish interests but also being inconsiderate and selfish with time and money.

Let's face our pride and selfishness, knowing that God will help us battle them and become more like Jesus.

Faulty Vision?

One of the problems with pride is that we can see it in others but not in ourselves.

Chapter 11, *Respectable Sins*

THINK IT THROUGH

For Personal Study

I. PRIDE OF SELF-RIGHTEOUSNESS

1. What does Scripture say about sinful pride (see James 4:6; 1 Peter 5:5) and the dangers that even believing teachers face (see Romans 2:1-3,21)?

2. "The sin of moral superiority and self-righteousness is so easy to fall into today," Jerry writes, "when society as a whole is openly committing or condoning such flagrant sins as immorality, easy divorce, a homosexual lifestyle, abortion. . . . Because we don't commit those sins, we tend to feel morally superior and look with a certain amount of disdain or contempt on those who do."

   a. Why do you suppose it is that we can so easily drift into the pride of moral superiority and then develop a spirit of contempt toward those who practice those sins?

b. To what kind of people did Jesus tell the parable about the self-righteous Pharisee? Why is this significant to us? (See Luke 18:9.)

3. Believers who care deeply about a particular belief system are susceptible to pride of correct doctrine — thinking that people who hold other beliefs are theologically or spiritually inferior. What did Paul say to prideful believers who concluded that eating food sacrificed to idols fell within the bounds of Christian liberty? (See 1 Corinthians 8:1.)

II. Pride of Achievement and Independence

1. Where does our ability to achieve or succeed come from? (See Genesis 45:4-8; 1 Samuel 2:7; Daniel 2:21; Haggai 1:5-6.)

2. Read 1 Corinthians 4:7. How relevant are Paul's words to us today? Why?

3. How does God feel about a proud heart? (See Psalm 101:5; Proverbs 16:5; 21:4.) How does He feel about our failure to acknowledge His gracious blessings?

4. Which biblical principles help us guard against a sinful desire for personal recognition? (See Luke 17:10; Psalm 75:6-7.)

5. What do Proverbs 2:1; 3:1; 4:1; 5:1; and 7:1 emphasize (in the context of a father-son relationship), and why are the principles of these verses relevant to the topic of prideful independence versus a teachable spirit?

III. THE SIN OF SELFISHNESS

1. What is the root of our selfishness? (See Genesis 3:1-6; Jeremiah 17:9; Hosea 6:7; Romans 7:17-20; 8:6-7; Galatians 5:16-17; Ephesians 2:3.)

2. Which phrase in 2 Timothy 3:1-2 describes a selfish person? Why is this so convicting?

3. Because time is precious, it's easy to be selfish with it. What do the following verses reveal about sharing our time with others? (See Acts 9:36; Romans 16:2; Galatians 5:13; 6:2; 1 Thessalonians 5:14; Hebrews 6:10; 1 Peter 4:10.)

4. In contrast to someone who is inconsiderate — not thinking about how what he or she says or does affects other people — what does God say about being considerate? (See Titus 3:1-2; James 3:17.)

Flesh Versus Spirit

We are born with a selfish nature. . . . Even after we become Christians, we still have the flesh that wars against the Spirit, and one of its expressions is selfishness.

Chapter 12, *Respectable Sins*

TALK IT OVER

For Group Discussion

1. Do you agree with the author that "there are degrees of selfishness as well as degrees of subtlety in expressing it"? Why or why not?

2. Have five group members each look up one of the following verses: Psalm 31:23; Jeremiah 50:31; Luke 1:51; Proverbs 8:13; and Proverbs 15:25. After each verse is read aloud, discuss together the passage's insight on how God feels about sinful pride.

3. Why does God hate sinful pride? How does it minimize His work in our lives?

4. Why is it sometimes difficult to focus on and listen to other people's interest areas rather than talking about our own? How do our selfish tendencies influence our conversations? Our activities? Our thoughts?

5. If we allow sinful pride and selfishness to take root in our lives, what consequences should we expect? (See 1 Corinthians 5:6.) Can you think of a time when you allowed this to happen? What did you experience as a result? How do you think other people felt about you?

6. Have three participants read aloud Romans 12:1-3; Philippians 2:3; and 1 Corinthians 13:4. After each verse, identify how God wants us to counter the sins of pride and selfishness.

GROUP PRAYER

Together, thank God for His blessings and ask Him for help in recognizing and dealing with the sins of pride and selfishness.

❧ ❧

FOR NEXT TIME: Read *Respectable Sins*, chapters 14, 15, and 16, and then respond to the "Think It Through" questions for session 6.

SELFISHNESS IS NOT LOVE

Love cares more for others than for self.
Love doesn't want what it doesn't have.
Love doesn't strut,
Doesn't have a swelled head,
Doesn't force itself on others,
Isn't always "me first,"
Doesn't fly off the handle,
Doesn't keep score of the sins of others,
Doesn't revel when others grovel.

1 Corinthians 13:4-6, MSG

****

TAKE IT TO HEART

A PERSONAL-GROWTH JOURNAL

PERSONAL REFLECTION

In which particular area(s) of your life do sinful expressions of pride and selfishness tend to surface (home, work, school, recreation, thoughts)?

Your conversations can reveal clues regarding pride and selfishness. As you converse with others, do you truly listen and empathize, or do you tend to shift the conversation to your own stories, interests, or achievements? Write down an example or two, followed by your thoughts on how God probably wanted you to behave.

What do your calendar and checkbook reveal about selfishness in your life?

Compare the sins of pride and selfishness to the fruit of the Spirit (see Galatians 5:22-23). What changes might you need to make, with the Holy Spirit's help?

PERSONAL ACTION POINT AND PRAYER

After you've identified areas of sinful pride and selfishness that may have taken root in your life, confess them to God in prayer. Ask Him to make you less mindful of yourself and more mindful of the needs of others.

****

Since the last session, did you catch pride and selfishness at work in your life? What brought it to your attention? How did you respond?

Why do you think pride and selfishness may be difficult to detect in ourselves?

As a result of your study of the "respectable" sins, how might your view of sin be changing?

Impatience, Irritability, and Anger

(Chapters 14, 15, and 16)

BEFORE GATHERING: Read *Respectable Sins* chapters 14, 15, and 16, and then respond to the "Think It Through" personal-study questions that begin on the next page.

KEY VERSES: "I . . . urge you to walk in a manner worthy of the calling to which you have been called, with all humility and gentleness, with patience. . . . I fear that perhaps when I come . . . there may be quarreling, jealousy, anger." (Ephesians 4:1-2; 2 Corinthians 12:20)

GET FOCUSED

Jim and Susan arrived at the restaurant ten minutes apart. "Well, you're late as always," he quipped.

"I'd have been on time," she retorted, eyes flashing, "if you hadn't left the car almost out of gas again."

Moments later, each of them stormed out. *I'll go work out,* Jim thought, *then get fast food.*

He's some piece of work, Susan muttered to herself. *He sleeps on the couch tonight.*

"Respectable" sins of impatience, irritability, and anger often surface among friends and family.

Impatience and irritability crop up easily, such as when we wait at the post office or a spouse or child consistently but unintentionally annoys us. It causes us to speak or behave in ways that hurt those we love and dishonor our Lord Jesus Christ.

Sinful anger can create even greater damage. We often ignore or deny this sin, so we'll focus on it a little more — and on its damaging offshoots, such as bitterness and strife.

According to Jerry Bridges, situations that arouse impatience, irritability, and anger can either drive us to sin or they can drive us to Christ and His sanctifying power. We must carefully determine ahead of time how we will respond when tempted to express impatience, irritability, and anger — and when people express them toward us. Will we vent our emotions with negative words, expressions, and body language? Or will we choose to trust in God's sovereignty, wisdom, and love? Big choices . . . with big consequences.

THINK IT THROUGH

For Personal Study

I. IMPATIENCE AND IRRITABILITY

1. Jerry defines *impatience* as "a strong sense of annoyance at the (usually) unintentional faults and failures of others." In what ways do you tend to express impatience? How do these expressions affect those people who are objects of your impatience?

2. Situations do not cause us to be impatient. "They merely provide," the author writes, "an opportunity for the flesh to assert itself. The actual cause of our impatience lies within our own hearts, in our own attitude of insisting that others around us conform to our expectations." Is Jerry's statement a new distinctive for you? Why is it important for us to understand this perspective?

3. Speaking through Paul in the Scriptures below, how does God want us to act when we're tempted to be impatient?

1 Corinthians 13:1,4:

Galatians 5:22-23:

Ephesians 4:1-2:

4. "*Irritability*," writes the author, "describes the frequency of impatience, or the ease with which a person can become impatient over the slightest provocation." Keeping Jerry's definition in mind, do you agree that irritability is a sin? What do you think lies at the root of the irritability? Be specific and explain your response.

Where Anger Comes From

No one else *causes* us to be angry. . . . The cause lies deep within us—usually our pride, or selfishness, or desire to control.
  Chapter 15, *Respectable Sins*

II. ANGER AND ITS "WEEDS"

1. Jerry defines anger as "a strong feeling of displeasure, and usually of antagonism . . . often accompanied by sinful emotions, words, and actions hurtful to those who are the objects of [the] anger." To what extent do you think anger has permeated our homes, friendships, and churches? Why?

2. Contrast what the Bible reveals about *righteous* anger with what it says about *sinful* anger:

a. Righteous anger (self-controlled, arises from an accurate perception of evil, focuses on God and His will):

Exodus 32:15-20:

Nehemiah 5:1-8:

Matthew 21:12-13:

b. Sinful anger (sinful reactions to people's actions and words):

Matthew 5:22:

Galatians 5:19-20:

Ephesians 4:29-31:

3. Read Ephesians 4:32 and Colossians 3:13. What guidance do these verses offer for guarding our attitude toward people whose words or actions tempt us to be impatient, irritable, and/or angry?

TALK IT OVER

For Group Discussion

1. Do you agree with the author that circumstances or people's actions can never *cause* us to be impatient, irritable, or angry? Explain your answer.

2. Discuss this statement: "We can choose how we will respond to the sinful actions of others toward us." Do you agree or disagree? Why?

3. What are the *real* causes of impatience, irritability, and sinful anger? Once we recognize them, what practical steps can we take to deal with them:

   a. *proactively* — before situations arise?

   b. *responsively* — in the heat-of-the-moment situation?

   c. *retrospectively* — once the Holy Spirit makes you aware that you've "blown it"?

4. Imagine that a good friend keeps justifying his or her sinful anger and refuses to face the deeper, causative issues. What might you say to him or her?

5. How has the sovereign God, in His wise and good purposes for you, used difficult situations (including impatient, irritable, and angry people) to teach you more about Him and the Christian life?

GROUP PRAYER

Ask God to help each of you, through the guidance of the Holy Spirit, to deal with impatience, irritability, and anger *proactively*, *responsively*, and *retrospectively* in the coming week.

❧ ❧

FOR NEXT TIME: Read *Respectable Sins*, chapters 17 and 19. Then respond to the "Think It Through" personal-study questions for session 7.

★★★★★★★★★★★★★★

Take It to Heart
A Personal-Growth Journal

Personal Reflection

Through your reading and study this week, what has God revealed to you about your tendencies to be impatient, irritable, or angry?

What commitment(s) are you willing to write down — right now — about how you intend to deal with these sins in the future? (Think proactively, responsively, and retrospectively.)

Personal Action Point and Prayer

Write out your heart's prayer, asking God to help you, through His Holy Spirit, to keep your proactive, responsive, and retrospective commitments when dealing with these "respectable" sins.

★★★★★★★★★★★★★★

BONUS STUDY

Battling Anger's "Noxious Weeds"

Long-term, unresolved anger creates many "noxious weeds" that poison lives. Use the following verses as a springboard to further explore the effects of these "weeds." Ask God to reveal any area in which He sees a weed growing in your life, and then recognize it and deal with it according to the guidance in the suggested Scripture references. If one or more of these conditions surfaces often — or in a way that leads to verbal or physical abuse of anyone — seek good Bible-based (pastoral) counseling.

Use the spaces below to note any personal tendencies God may be revealing to you. Summarize His message to you in the corresponding Scriptures.

RESENTMENT — internalized, unresolved anger that is held onto. *(See 1 Corinthians 13:5; 2 Timothy 2:22-24.)*

BITTERNESS — resentment that has grown into ongoing animosity. *(See Romans 3:12-14; James 3:14.)*

HOLDING A GRUDGE — taking revenge on the object of the grudge. *(See Romans 12:18-21; James 5:9.)*

STRIFE — open conflict or turmoil between people. *(See Proverbs 30:33; Romans 1:29; 1 Timothy 6:3-4.)*

BONUS STUDY

Learning to Forgive

Read Jesus' parable of the unforgiving servant in Matthew 18:21-35. Then respond thoughtfully, in writing, to the following prompts:

From the parable, what can we learn about forgiving others as God has forgiven us?

Every sin we commit, regardless of how insignificant it seems to us, is an assault on God's infinite glory. What did it cost God to forgive us?

How should we then live?

How should we then forgive others?

Anger is never static. If it is not dealt with, it will grow into bitterness, hostility, and revenge-minded grudges.

Chapter 16, *Respectable Sins*

Since the last session, when have impatience or anger surfaced in your life? In the lives of people around you? How did you respond?

What is at the root of irritability, and what impact does it have on those around us? Have you been more aware of it this week than before? Why or why not?

Together, review ways in which each of us can deal more effectively with such sins through the power of the Holy Spirit.

Judgmentalism and Sins of the Tongue

(Chapters 17 and 19)

BEFORE GATHERING: Read *Respectable Sins*, chapters 17 and 19, and then respond to the "Think It Through" personal-study questions that begin on the next page of this guide.

KEY VERSES: "There is only one lawgiver and judge, he who is able to save and to destroy. But who are you to judge your neighbor? . . . Let no corrupting talk come out of your mouths, but only such as is good for building up, as fits the occasion, that it may give grace to those who hear." (James 4:12; Ephesians 4:29)

GET FOCUSED

If you were to gather one hundred church people from a variety of ages and lifestyles and ask which type of church music is best and what the "dress code" of a church should be, disagreement would erupt. Why? Because we often equate our opinions with truth and quickly judge people who disagree with us. This leads to the "respectable" sin of judgmentalism. "How easy it is," Jerry Bridges writes, "to become judgmental over issues the Bible does not address or address with the clarity we would like."

As we'll realize during this session, personal preferences are quite different from Bible-based convictions and God's clear commands. Clearly there are moments where it is best to agree to disagree. For example, the Bible doesn't tell us what kind of music to listen to. And when we need to humbly defend key biblical doctrines and challenge believers whose lifestyle or conduct is clearly out of line with the Bible, we need to avoid demonizing or becoming hypercritical of those with whom we disagree.

Playing God

If I'm correct, then the seriousness of the sin of judgmentalism is not so much that I judge my brother as that in so doing I assume the role of God.

Chapter 17, *Respectable Sins*

"Respectable" sins of the tongue — gossip, negative words, slander, and so on — are also common within the church and our culture. Even though they are often tolerated and even encouraged, these sins are incredibly damaging. Fortunately God gives His followers His power so we can "put on our new selves" — created after His likeness in true righteousness and holiness.

THINK IT THROUGH

For Personal Study

I. JUDGMENTALISM

1. "Judgmentalism begins," writes the author, when "we equate our opinions with truth." What's the difference between a preference for something (a certain kind of food, for example) and a Bible-based conviction? What can happen when we elevate personal convictions concerning an issue to the level of biblical truth — even when the Bible is not clear on that particular issue?

2. "It is easy," the author writes, "to become judgmental toward anyone whose opinions are different from ours." Think of a time when you've seen this happen. What consequences occurred?

3. Paul faced judgmentalism head-on (see Romans 14). One group in the church at Rome ate only vegetables and thought they had the moral high ground (see 14:3); another group ate "anything" (presumably meat) and thought they had superior knowledge because what they ate made no difference to God if it was received with thanksgiving (1 Timothy 4:4). And each group judged the other. In addition, some believers observed certain days as holy days, and other believers did not.

a. Read Romans 14:4-5. How would you describe Paul's response?

b. What position did Paul take concerning the personal convictions of what people ate or special days they observed?

4. "Because we do believe so strongly in the importance of sound doctrine," Jerry writes, "we can easily become hypercritical of those with whom we disagree." What do you think is the proper balance between (a) standing up for key biblical doctrine, and (b) expressing disagreement with advocates of unsound doctrine in ways that do not degenerate into character assassination?

II. SINS OF THE TONGUE

1. How do we know that God takes "respectable" sins of the tongue seriously? (See Matthew 12:36-37.)

2. "Any speech," the author writes, "that tends to tear down another person — either someone we are talking about or someone we are talking to — is sinful speech." Do you agree or disagree? Why?

3. Read Ephesians 4:29. Describe, in your own words, what God (through Paul) tells us to do. How does this verse relate to the "put off/put on" principle Paul mentioned earlier in verses 22-24?

4. Which word picture(s) did James use (see James 3:1-12) to illustrate the tongue's power and sinful effects? What did he want us to realize?

TALK IT OVER

For Group Discussion

1. Biblically, when should we pass judgment on the practices and beliefs of other believers? What criteria must we use? (Read Romans 1:24-32; Galatians 5:19-21; 2 Timothy 3:1-5.) How is the perspective of Bible-based confrontation different from much of our society's emphasis on "tolerance"?

2. What dangers do we face when we judge others whose preferences and practices are different from ours? When do we need to pass Bible-based judgment on the practices and beliefs of a believer whose lifestyle or conduct is clearly not in line with the Scriptures?

3. How have Christians' judgmentalism and sinful speech affected their churches? Their witness in the local community?

4. Jerry writes: "Note Paul's absolute prohibition [in Ephesians 4:29]. *No* corrupting talk. None whatsoever. This means *no* gossip, *no* sarcasm, *no* critical speech, *no* harsh words. . . . Think about what the church of Jesus Christ would look like if we all sought to apply Paul's words." If indeed we could live and worship together in this way, what *would* the body of Christ be like? What are we each willing to do in order to help make that happen?

5. How can we disagree strongly with people who undermine key biblical doctrine, such as Jesus' substitutionary atonement for our sins, while not committing judgmentalism?

6. What is the real problem and source of our sinful speech? (See Matthew 12:33; Luke 6:45.)

GROUP PRAYER

As a group, pray together this prayer of David (Psalm 19:14): "Let the words of my mouth and the meditation of my heart be acceptable in your sight, O LORD, my rock and my redeemer."

❧ ☙

FOR NEXT TIME: Read *Respectable Sins*, chapters 13 and 18, and then respond to the "Think It Through" personal-study questions for session 8.

†††††††††††††††

Take It to Heart
A Personal-Growth Journal

Personal Reflection

How do you feel when you are with someone who continually practices judgmentalism — having a critical spirit and finding fault with everyone and everything? Why do you think a critical spirit is so damaging?

Which sins of the tongue tempt you the most?

"The tongue," writes the author, "is only the instrument that reveals what's in our hearts." Based on your speech, what is in your heart? What might the Holy Spirit be prompting you to do about it?

Personal Action Point

For the next two days, ask yourself, Will what I'm about to say tend to tear down or build up the person to whom I speak (or about whom I speak)?

Personal Prayer

Confess any sins of judgmentalism or sins of the tongue. Talk honestly with God about how you'd like to improve, and invite Him to help you.

★★★★★★★★★★★★★★

How aware are you becoming of your "respectable" sins, including judgmentalism and sins of the tongue?

What are you willing to do in order to remain focused on these types of sins now that this study is drawing to a close? What benefits will you receive if you do this — spiritually, relationally, vocationally?

Share one "take-away" that has affected you the most during the previous seven sessions, and why it is so significant.

Which key Scripture or important principle from this study might you share with other people?

Lack of Self-Control, Envy, and Jealousy

(Chapters 13 and 18)

BEFORE GATHERING: Read *Respectable Sins*, chapters 13 and 18, and then respond to the "Think It Through" personal-study questions that begin on the next page of this guide.

KEY VERSES: "A man without self-control is like a city broken into and left without walls. . . . The works of the flesh are evident: . . . jealousy, fits of anger, rivalries, dissensions, divisions, envy." (Proverbs 25:28; Galatians 5:19-21)

GET FOCUSED

Self-control is unpopular in many circles. Our culture offers many temptations and encourages us to fulfill our desires. *Go ahead, experience it. Buy it. Try it. It's your right. You've earned it.*

Through words and personal examples, the Bible says much about self-control. Solomon backslid horribly because he lacked self-control. Other biblical characters lost their tempers, ate to excess during Communion-related meals, and became materialistic. As believers, we experience passions of the flesh that wage war against our souls (see 1 Peter 2:11).

Most of us recognize boundaries that tend to restrain us from obvious sins, but otherwise we pretty much live as we please. Knowing it is easy for us to say yes instead of no, and indulge sinful desires, God emphasizes self-control repeatedly. It is even listed in the fruit of the Spirit (see Galatians 5:22-23). You see, this self-control is not control by our own willpower, but rather control of ourselves through the Holy Spirit's power.

What Is Self-Control?

Self-control . . . is a governance or prudent control of one's desires, cravings, impulses, emotions, and passions. It is saying no when we should say no. It is moderation in legitimate desires and activities, and absolute restraint in areas that are clearly sinful.

Chapter 13, *Respectable Sins*

Since humankind's earliest days, envy, jealousy, and related sins — such as sinful competitiveness and trying to control people — have caused great problems. For example, jealous Cain killed Abel (see Genesis 4:1-8). It's easy to respond with envy and jealousy when people enjoy advantages and blessings we don't have, to compare ourselves to others whose circumstances, talents, and giftedness seem better than ours. And to ignore how vile envy and jealousy really are (see Romans 1:29; Galatians 5:20-21).

THINK IT THROUGH

For Personal Study

I. LACK OF SELF-CONTROL

1. A person lacking self-control is vulnerable to all kinds of temptations. Solomon, who wrote a key verse found at the beginning of this session, illustrates this. What happened to him and the Israelite nation, as recorded in 1 Kings 11:1-6,29-33?

2. What do these verses reveal to you about self-control?

Galatians 5:22-23:

2 Timothy 3:1-3:

Titus 2:2,5-6:

Ecclesiastes 2:10:

3. Because biblical self-control is not a product of our natural will-power, what trains us to live self-controlled lives? (See Titus 2:11-12.) What does this insight mean to you personally?

4. In order for us to exercise self-control, what must we battle unceasingly? (See 1 Peter 2:11.)

5. "Self-control is dependent," Jerry writes, "on the influence and enablement of the Holy Spirit. It requires continual exposure of our mind to the words of God and continual prayer for the Holy Spirit to give us both the desire and power to exercise self-control."

a. In our individualistic, goal-oriented culture, why is this truth important to remember?

b. In light of our busy lives, what specific steps can we take to ensure that we expose our minds continually to God's Word? That we pray regularly and draw closer to God?

II. ENVY AND JEALOUSY

1. What points did Paul make about envy and jealousy in:

Romans 1:28-29?

1 Corinthians 13:4?

Galatians 5:19-21?

2. Read these verses and make note of the kinds of things that tempt people to become envious and jealous:

Acts 5:12-17; 13:44-45:

_____

What Are Envy and Jealousy?

1 Samuel 18:6-9:

Envy is the painful and oftentimes resentful awareness of an advantage enjoyed by someone else. . . . We tend to envy those with whom we most closely identify. . . . [and] envy in them the areas we value most. _Jealousy_ . . . is intolerance of rivalry. Sinful jealousy occurs when we are afraid someone is going to become equal to or even superior to us.

Genesis 4:4-8; 37:4-11,18-20:

Chapter 18, _Respectable Sins_

_____

Esther 5:9-13:

3. Jerry writes, "Closely allied with envy and jealousy is the spirit of competitiveness — the urge to always win or be the top person in whatever our field of endeavor is." What's the difference between doing our best and being driven by envy and jealousy?

Doing Our Best: See 2 Timothy 2:15; Colossians 3:23; 1 Corinthians 9:24-27.

Being Driven by Envy or Jealousy: See Ecclesiastes 4:4; Song of Songs 8:6; James 3:16.

BONUS ACTION POINTS

Facing Up to Envy or Jealousy

When we are tempted to be envious or jealous, we can:

1. Remind ourselves of God's sovereignty. He gives us our talents, abilities, spiritual gifts, and opportunities (see 1 Samuel 2:7). To be envious or jealous of someone either eliminates God from the picture or accuses Him of being unfair.

2. Remember that all believers are "one body in Christ" and that each member of that body "belongs to all the others" (Romans 12:5, NIV). So, as Paul put it, "Outdo one another in showing honor" (Romans 12:10). Instead of being envious or jealous, let's honor and applaud people because we are all members of the same body in Christ. Let's submit to each other (see Ephesians 5:21).

3. Know that God has a place and assignment for each of us that He wants us to fill, and admittedly some of us garner more human recognition than others. If we spend emotional energy on envy or jealousy, we lose sight of what God might do uniquely in our lives. All assignments are important in God's plan.

TALK IT OVER
For Group Discussion

1. What kind of self-control, envy, and jealousy temptations do you face? What are some signals that we lack self-control, that our sinful desires are either starting to control us or have been controlling us?

2. What would you say are the three biggest areas in which people fail to exercise self-control? How can we recognize these temptations more quickly? What are the consequences? Practically speaking, how can we increase self-control when we are tempted to indulge our desires?

3. In his book, the author shares how a seemingly benign practice greatly weakened his self-control in more critical areas. In which areas are you tempted to use less self-control and give in to your desires?

4. Discuss this quote from chapter 13: "We cannot pick and choose the areas of life in which we will exercise self-control."

5. "Sinful jealousy occurs," writes the author, "when we are afraid someone is going to become equal to or even superior to us." Can you think of examples of this kind of jealousy? Why do you think it is displeasing to God?

6. If God is sovereign over the abilities and blessings He's given us, how should this truth influence our tendencies toward envy and sinful jealousy?

GROUP PRAYER

Confess that you need God and His truth in order to vigilantly deal with "respectable" sins. Thank Him for His Holy Spirit, who lives within every believer and provides the power necessary to resist sin and draw closer to God. Pray for specific people in your group who have shared particular struggles. Close by affirming who God is and who He calls each believer to be.

BONUS STUDY

Good Jealousy?

Did you realize that not all jealousy is sinful? Being intolerant of rivalry can be godly. For example, if you are married and someone tries to win your spouse away from you, you feel legitimate jealousy. God, who declares Himself to be a jealous God, will not tolerate the worship of anyone or anything other than Him. Explore what the Bible says about God's jealousy:

Exodus 20:5:

Psalm 78:58:

Zechariah 1:14:

1 Corinthians 10:21-22:

ﻬﻬﻬﻬﻬﻬﻬﻬﻬﻬﻬ

Take It to Heart

A Personal-Growth Journal

Personal Reflection

Reread the definition of self-control. Does lack of self-control keep surfacing in your life? If so, in which area(s)?

What role might the Holy Spirit play in helping you exercise more self-control?

Write out your response to this question: Is envy or sinful jealousy worth the energy? Explain your response.

If God were to underline any parts of this session with you in mind, what might He mark? Why?

Personal Action Point

After rereading the definitions of self-control, envy, and jealousy, contemplate areas where they may have made inroads into your life. How do you plan to make progress over these "respectable" sins?

Personal Prayer

Thank God for what you have learned during these sessions and ask for the will and power to keep dealing with "respectable" sins and pursuing the path He has for you.

ﻬﻬﻬﻬﻬﻬﻬﻬﻬﻬﻬ

Take It to Heart

A Personal-Growth Journal

Wrapping It Up

Think back on your personal study and group discussions of *Respectable Sins: Confronting the Sins We Tolerate*. Identify three key discoveries or principles that stood out to you regarding God's view of the "respectable" sins, our tendencies to commit and overlook these sins, or God's provision for overcoming these sins. What comes to mind?

1.

2.

3.

Think back on any life-change commitments you prayed about during the past several weeks. What were they, and how are you doing in living out those commitments? (Use the next page if needed.)

Think back on a personal victory you may have experienced over one of the "respectable" sins in recent weeks. Use this space to recount the story. Conclude by commenting on how it felt (and feels) to win over sin in that particular situation. (Use the next page if needed.)

What would you like to tell or ask God right now regarding "respectable" sins in your life? Write out your prayer as if He's reading over your shoulder. Don't forget to express your dependence on and trust in Him to help you lead the godly life He desires for you. (Use the next page if needed.)

Author

JERRY BRIDGES is an author and Bible teacher. His most popular book, *The Pursuit of Holiness*, has sold over one million copies. He is also the author of *Trusting God*, *The Discipline of Grace*, *The Practice of Godliness*, *The Fruitful Life*, and *The Gospel for Real Life*. As a full-time staff member with The Navigators for many years, Jerry has served in the collegiate ministry and community ministries.

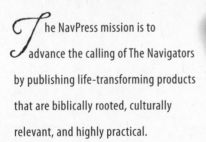

SUPPORT THE MINISTRY OF THE NAVIGATORS

The Navigators' calling is to advance the gospel of Jesus and His kingdom into the nations through spiritual generations of laborers living and discipling among the lost.

Navigators have invested their lives in people for more than 75 years, coming alongside them life on life to help them passionately know Christ and to make Him known.

The U.S. Navigators' ministry touches lives in varied settings, including college campuses, military bases, downtown offices, urban neighborhoods, prisons, and youth camps.

Dedicated to helping people navigate spiritually, The Navigators aims to make a permanent difference in the lives of people around the world. The Navigators helps its communities of friends to follow Christ passionately and equip them effectively to go out and do the same.

To learn more about donating to The Navigators' ministry,
go to **www.navigators.org/us/support**
or call toll-free at **1-866-568-7827**.

THE NAVIGATORS®